FLYING FOXES

EMILY RAABE

The Rosen Publishing Group's
PowerKids Press™
New York

For Lorenzo

Published in 2003 by The Rosen Publishing Group, Inc.
29 East 21st Street, New York, NY 10010

First Edition

Editor: Natashya Wilson
Book Design: Emily Muschinske

Photo Credits: Cover, title page, pp. 6, 12 © Michael Durham; pp. 4, 7, 10, 11, 17, 21 (inset) © Robert and Linda Mitchell; pp. 5, 15 © Merlin D. Tuttle, Bat Conservation International; p. 9 © Hans & Judy Beste/Animals Animals; p. 9 (map) Eric Dipalo; pp. 12 (inset), 13, 18, 21 © Albert Visage/Peter Arnold; p. 16 © Oregon Zoo; p. 19 © Roland Seitre/Peter Arnold, Inc.; p. 22 © Steven David Miller/Animals Animals.

Raabe, Emily.
Flying foxes / Emily Raabe.— 1st ed.
   p. cm. — (The library of bats)
Summary: An introduction to the flying fox, a type of bat that belongs to the relatively uncommon Megachiroptera order.
ISBN 0-8239-6324-1 (library binding)
1. Flying foxes—Juvenile literature. [1. Flying foxes. 2. Bats.] I. Title. II. Series.
QL737.C575 R235 2003
599.4'9—dc21
                                        2001005334

Manufactured in the United States of America

CONTENTS

HAND-WING FLIERS

Scientists sort all animals into groups called **orders**. Bats belong to the order Chiroptera (ky-RAHP-truh). This word comes from the Greek words meaning "hand" and "wing." Scientists group bats again by breaking the order Chiroptera into two smaller orders. These two orders are the Microchiroptera (MY-kroh-ky-rahp-truh), or small bats, and the Megachiroptera (MEH-guh-ky-rahp-truh), or large bats. Almost all the bats in the world are Microchiroptera bats. Only flying foxes and some kinds of fruit bats are Megachiroptera bats. As real foxes are, flying foxes are furry and have big eyes. They can be black, silver, red, gray, brown, yellow, or even orange!

This gray-headed flying fox is dining on the flowers of a black bean tree. You can see where the skin of the bat's wing stretches from shoulder to thumb. ➡

BAT FACT

Bats' hands really are their wings! Bats have very long fingers. A layer of skin is stretched like webbing between their fingers. Skin also stretches from bats' shoulders to their thumbs. The above picture shows the long, clawed thumb of a giant flying fox. Bats' skin makes their hands into wings. The skin is made of two layers.

MEGABATS

Have you ever seen a bat swooping around in your backyard? If you have, then chances are that you have seen a Microchiroptera bat. These microbats, as they are sometimes called, are the kinds of bats with which most people are familiar. Megachiroptera bats, or megabats, are not the bats you usually see. For one thing, megabats are big. Microbats weigh from $\frac{1}{20}$ of an ounce to 7 ounces (1.5–198 g). Megabats weigh from $\frac{2}{5}$ of an ounce to 56 ounces (11–1,588 g)! Another difference between the two types of bats is diet. Unlike microbats, which eat mostly insects, megabats eat mostly fruit.

BAT FACT

Dawn cave bats *(above)* are unusual megabats, because they live in caves. Most megabats live in trees. Microbats live in caves or in buildings. They fly only at night. Microbats also hibernate, or go into a deep sleep, during winter. Megabats fly around during the day, and they do not hibernate.

Rodgriguez flying foxes wrap and flap their wings. This type of flying fox is in danger of dying out.

WHERE CAN YOU FIND A FLYING FOX?

Most flying foxes live near water, and many of them live on islands. Flying foxes live in Australia, India, Pakistan, Nepal, Burma, Southeast Asia, the Philippines, Indonesia, southern Japan, and on islands in the Indian Ocean and the western Pacific Ocean. They sleep in trees and bushes, so you can often find them in woods or in brushy areas. They also like swamps. Living in swamps helps to protect flying foxes from animals that want to eat them. If you are in an area where flying foxes live, you might hear them before you see them.

Flying foxes are very noisy! As you get close, you will see what looks like hundreds of large birds hanging upside down from tree branches. These "birds" are flying foxes.

BAT STATS

Flying foxes have more than 30 different types of calls that they make to "talk" to one another. These calls range from the squeaking of babies to the screaming of fighting adult flying foxes.

This black flying fox lives in New Guinea. The map (inset) shows where flying foxes live throughout the world.

FLYING FOX
HOMES

Bats Are Not Blind!

Remember that old saying "blind as a bat?" Forget about it! All bats can see, and flying foxes can see better than most of them. Flying foxes see about as well as house cats. This means that in daylight, their vision is just a little bit worse than average human vision. In low light, however, their vision is much better than ours. Most bats use a special tool called **echolocation** to help them find their way in the dark. Echolocation is a way of bouncing a sound off of an object and listening to how long it takes for the sound to come back. Flying foxes do not echolocate. Instead they use their vision and their great senses of smell to find their food.

Bat Fact

Flying foxes' eyes are set in the fronts of their faces. This tells scientists that vision is important to flying foxes. Animals with eyes on the sides of their heads usually rely more on other senses, such as smell or hearing. Flying foxes' hearing is about the same as humans' hearing. This means that flying foxes do not hear as well as do many other animals.

Flying foxes are the only bats that can see in color. This color vision helps them to find the kinds of flowers and fruits they like to eat.

AMAZING WINGS

Flying foxes are strong fliers. They can fly from 15 ½ to 18 ½ miles per hour (25–30 km/h) for up to four hours without taking a rest. This is even more amazing when you know that flying foxes do not take breaks by **gliding** on the wind the way that most birds do. Flying foxes flap their wings for almost the entire time that they are flying. Their wings have other uses, too. If the weather is cold, a flying fox's wings become a handy blanket. If it is raining, flying foxes use their wings like raincoats and wrap themselves up to stay dry. Flying foxes can also swim very well. They use their wings like paddles to move through the water.

BAT FACT

Flying foxes' legs do not have much muscle on them, as do our legs. Having bulky muscles would make flying foxes too heavy to fly. Instead their legs work like strong ropes. They are not any good for walking, but they are great for hanging upside down!

A flying fox opens its strong wing. The Malayan flying fox (inset) has the largest wingspan of all bats.

Hunting for Flowers

Most bats eat insects. Some bats eat mice and other **rodents**. Some bats eat fish. Some bats eat other bats, and some bats eat blood. Flying foxes eat flower parts, fruit juices, and fruit. In fact flying foxes are one of the most important ways in which many trees and flowers of the rain forest **reproduce**. In the rain forest, many different kinds of trees live side by side in mixed groups. Yet to reproduce, a tree needs to get **pollen** from a tree that is the same kind as itself. Trees might grow too far away to share pollen. Flying foxes fly long distances with grains of pollen clinging to their fur. When flying foxes feed, the pollen falls off their fur and spreads to other trees. This is how many rain forest trees get **pollinated** and are able to reproduce.

Bat Stats

Flying foxes are bigger than most other bats. Malayan flying foxes have the biggest wings of all bats. Their wingspans can be as much as 5 ½ feet (1.5 m) long!

This black flying fox has landed on a red bottle brush plant.

BAT FACT

How in the world do flying foxes go to the bathroom if they are hanging upside down from their feet? First they flip around on their branch so that they are hanging right side up by their thumbs. Then they do their business, give a small shake, and flip back upside down!

Flying foxes live in camps. Camps are groups of flying foxes all living in the same group of trees or bushes. They hang from the branches in noisy groups. Flying foxes often move their camps to be near certain fruits or flowers when they blossom. In the summer, male and female flying foxes live in the same camps. Summer camps can be made up of as many as 250,000 flying foxes. In the winter, camps are much smaller and quieter. Most winter camps are groups of females only or groups of males only. If the winter is a hard one, flying foxes might move their camps many times to find food.

Flying foxes help trees by pollinating them, but they can also hurt trees by living in them. The weight of so many flying foxes can break a tree's branches and can kill it.

FLYING FOX BABIES

Flying fox females have babies at two years old. They have one baby each year. The females are very good mothers. The babies are born with very little hair, so the mothers wrap them up in a wing to keep them warm. For the first three weeks, the mothers carry their babies everywhere with them. After three weeks, the babies are left together in camp while the mothers look for food. After six weeks, the babies begin to practice flapping their wings. At about four months of age, the young bats form groups of their own. Male flying foxes take the young flying foxes on trips to teach them how to find food.

BAT FACT

Flying fox babies begin to learn to fly when they are about three months old. This is a very noisy time in the camps. Baby flying foxes return from short flights and crash into trees all over the place! After the babies crash, they sit and call for their mothers. When a mother hears her baby calling, she calls back until her baby finds her.

 While female flying foxes are pregnant, they separate themselves from the males. The females hang upside down together and groom one another.

DANGER FOR THE FLYING FOX

Flying foxes can live up to 30 years, but many of them die earlier than this. Crocodiles, large snakes, sea eagles, and owls are all **predators** of flying foxes. However, the biggest danger to flying foxes is human beings. In some places, such as the island of Guam, flying foxes are hunted and are eaten by humans. In some places, people believe that their skin can help sick people to get well. In many places, flying foxes are killed by people who see them as pests that destroy trees and eat fruit from orchards. Many flying foxes are also killed each year when they collide with power lines. In Australia, power companies have begun to wrap power lines in protective covering to protect flying foxes. Flying foxes can also be killed by getting tangled in **barbed wire** fences.

BAT STATS

Most flying fox camps have at least one python snake living nearby, waiting to catch and to eat unlucky flying foxes.

Flying foxes are in constant danger from people. They need to stay alert.

SAVING FLYING FOXES

Scientists are working hard to teach people about the importance of flying foxes. Without flying foxes spreading seeds and pollen, many trees and plants might die out. Because of the work of these scientists, people in areas where flying foxes live are beginning to work to protect them. People in places, such as Samoa and other islands in the South Pacific, where the flying fox **populations** have almost disappeared, have begun to stop hunting flying foxes. They have also begun to set aside land where flying foxes can live in safety. Today people are beginning to change their thinking about these amazing bats.

BAT FACT

Thousands of gray-headed flying foxes live for part of the year in Australia's Royal Melbourne Botanic Gardens. The garden keepers knew the bats might kill the rare trees. In 2001, they decided to kill 1,000 flying foxes. People complained. Now scientists and garden keepers are working together to save both the bats and the trees.

GLOSSARY

barbed wire (BARBD WYR) Metal wire with sharp, jagged points, used to make fences.

echolocation (eh-koh-loh-KAY-shun) A method of locating objects by producing a sound and judging the time it takes the echo to return and the direction from which it returns. Bats, dolphins, porpoises, killer whales, and some shrews all use echolocation.

gliding (GLYD-ing) Floating without using any energy.

orders (OR-durz) Scientific groupings of plants or animals that are alike in some ways.

pollen (PAH-lin) Yellow, powdery grains made by the male part of flowers.

pollinated (PAH-lih-nayt-id) When a plant receives pollen from another plant so that the plants can multiply.

populations (pah-pyoo-LAY-shunz) The numbers of any one kind of creature living in a place.

predators (PREH-duh-terz) Animals that eat other animals for food.

reproduce (ree-pruh-DOOS) To bear young or offspring.

rodents (ROH-dints) Animals with gnawing teeth, such as mice.

INDEX

WEB SITES

To learn more about flying foxes, check out these Web sites:

http://online.anu.edu.au/srmes/wildlife/batatlas/at_foxes.html
www.bellingen.com/flyingfoxes/
www.pbs.org/kratts/world/aust/flyingfox/index.html